Ghost and Spirit

S.F. Begum

BookLeaf Publishing
India | USA | UK

Presentation by *BookLeaf Publishing*

Web: www.bookleafpub.com

E-mail: info@bookleafpub.com

ISBN: 9789357444828

First edition 2022

DEDICATION

To all the souls who've ever felt too much and too little - sometimes at the same time.

You're always enough.

ACKNOWLEDGEMENT

This book would not exist without the loving-
and often sarcastic and/or blunt- advice of my
siblings, Nili, Muntaha, and Iram, who patiently
read and reflect on every writing piece I show
them. Many thanks to my dear friends Emily
Singh and Mallory Koomen who have
introduced me to this opportunity and helped me
organize this book, (as well as also patiently
read and reflect on every writing piece I show
them).
BookLeaf Publishing, I am forever thankful for
you providing the platform and opportunity for
my work. Aayushi Thapa, as my publishing
consultant, I am so very appreciative of your
time, patience, and support in the process of
bringing this book to life.
And for their unrelenting love, support, and
everything else really, thank you always to my
parents, Rowshon Ara Begum and Saied Belal.

Cycles

The mosquito lovingly nestles on my forearm
and pierces my skin
in a quiet kiss

It won't take much,
just leave with its fill
It's not enough to be missed

And the bird consumes the bug
and I consume the bird
and fall to the earth,
consumed by the dirt

And all in the world consume one another
become one another
return to one another

And all in the world fall in love with one another
We're each other's death,
and each other's birth.

To live

Let us fall in love
before the stars in our eyes burn up
before they cool
shrink
turn white and black with the humdrum of the
day
and then fade from existence

Let us feed them
let us grow

Let us take up so much space
that space itself is suffocated
Let us feel the burning fury of a thousand suns
so when the stars' time has come,
may they die with the magnificence of a
supernova

Let us dance in the rain
before our feet are bound to desks and duties
before we gain a sense of reserve and
preservation
that restrain our will and whimsy

Let us waltz
let us sing

Let the damp unforgiving concrete of reality
become the dance floor upon which we pave our
dreams
Let freedom be the iron shoes we wear until we
perish
so when the time comes for us,
we'll have been truly and utterly free

Let us fly
in the only way that humans can
with leaping hearts and euphoric wings

And so by fly, let us love
let us soar

For the same reason we whisper our prayers and
wishes
and we close our eyes when we kiss
and why our breath catches at the sight of life
breaking into a new day
Living is the most intimate kind of love
So before this world takes us and breaks us,
let us fall in love.

Participation Award

I live on the edge of a cliff
that looks like a pedestal
the farther you step away

And every step is potential death
so I've stopped walking
And every breath is an elevated retch
so I've stopped talking
And if the Realm of Forms isn't in my sight
then I'm not trying,
For I won't take risks
when flying can mean dying

And I'm frozen by fear
and yearn for plateaus
where being is okay

Where I can live in my form
without climbing higher
Where love and growth come naturally
without achievement hard-wired
And I can be both the norm and particular
without shame resisting,
For I want to exist,
and celebrate existing.

Clouds

I used to think that
I had to hide under an umbrella
Live in pockets of dryness,
untouched, unaffected
And yet how the drops became puddles
and puddles became ponds
And so I became too
a madman, inflicted

And then I was the umbrella
shielding others from the sky's grief
As they raged, I stood tall,
unflinching, enduring
But the ponds flowed into streams
and my muffles turned into screams
And they flowed into one consciousness
of a lonely soul, yearning

And now I realize
That I am the clouds
I'll pour my heart out
unrelenting, undenying
My raindrops are what elevate me,
my thunder emancipates me
You say I am vulnerable,

I say I am flying.

Holding Night

Have you heard her steps last night,
her gentle stroking of your hair?
Has she grazed your jugular
and released a puff of air?

Has she sunk her fingers deep
and wrenched your consciousness from you?
Did you fade as she held your gaze?
Have you fallen last night too?

"It won't happen again. I'll be vigilant."
But alas you have no say
You can run from space but not from time
and at night she'll have her way

Lover or reaper, you can choose her name,
but not her final decree
Will her embrace only last the night
or for eternity?

An Elusive Guest

I'm uncomfortable around Death
I never know what to say
They're a vision beyond my periphery
an end-
　invisible,

　　　　　　intangible

The unforgiving magnitude by which they
upheave lives
has always lived a block

　　　　　　　　　　too far

for me to feel the seismic waves

Yet Death has lived near me

They rest in the shadows beyond my mother's
eyes
and live in the pauses between my father's
words,
lie with all the things he doesn't say

Death took my mother's father before she knew
his face
and took my father's mother from his very arms

Took too many people for me to know their
names
and in their place, left silence and qualms

And so Death lives close
softer than a whisper
the ghost of a ghost

I wonder the name of a pain that exists without
memory
And I wonder if we can mourn what we never
knew
Perhaps its name is regret
And perhaps regret is mourning the tomorrow
that could have been

Yet, I am fortunate and I know
this will not always be the case
One day, Death will knock at my door
or of a loved one close by
and ask for some sugar
And we'll likely be unprepared
perhaps just putting a child to sleep or heading
out for work
or out back gardening, planting seeds for a
future now bathed in shadows

Or perhaps we'll be waiting

Perhaps Death called beforehand and so we sat
by the clock,
enjoying one last home baked muffin,
one last beloved's kiss,
heart in our mouths beating with the ticks of the
second hand
until that fateful knock…

I hope, until then,
I can walk the tranquil land graced by those who
passed
And when I finally meet that elusive guest, I can
tell them
that they're welcome to my home.

Treading, Untethered

You tread in the waters
past the near shore,
sand imprinting your journey
-momentarily

The waves tug at your shirt
-they want you to play-
and all of your weight,
they'll carry

But the rocks in your chest
they tether you down
and your bones, they are so weary

You think back on the days,
you were an anchor once,
carried many a boat and ferry

Yet now you walk on
free of your bounds
free of your bonds

You're free to float
you're free to fly
you're free to be and not to be
free to feel and free to see
that freedom's other name-

is lonely.

Honey

I love honey
not just for how it tastes
but for how it makes me feel

Its touch, sticky and all-consuming,
its weight on my tongue,
and the way it embraces the light to create its
own glow

I love it with my chamomile tea
when the world and my head feel heavy
and I need something sweet

How it clears my skin,
compliments my day
How it makes any meal feel complete

Honey, I love you
not just for how you make me feel
but for who you are

Your touch, gentle and loving
the weight of your hand in mine

And the way you light up my world much more
than you know.

Inheritance

You ask me why there are mountains between us
and I try to answer
but there's gravel in my mouth
chipped from the years
I had to swallow my pride

And you reach your hand forward
to rest on my shoulder
but it's hardened, no longer
a valley you can rest
my dear one, it's hollow inside

Your eyes ask what's wrong
the words only echo in my ears
they're caverns, sounds have no meaning
I could not take your false truths
so silence is how I defied

You don't recall what you did
just see what I am now
You say I am cold
yet you were the one
who held out my wrists
and poured ice in my veins

until numbness became a mercy

so if my heart is frozen
you have yourself to blame
my words are unspoken
for I choose not to defame
and I do not embrace you
because I am in pain

I inherited this pain
from you

but I put down my backpack
and made my own valley
for I won't pass on
this inheritance too.

Ragdoll

If I were a ragdoll,
I'd trace the edge of my ribs, take a
seam ripper
 and undo myself stitch by stitch

I'd sink my hand in my chest,
efficient and curt, fingers searching,
asking,
where does it hurt?

fluff insulation unwoven,
my insides would scream, howl
like the wind
being robbed of its dream

would cry like the moon
after losing its light,
would shiver like the earth
in perpetual night,
would gasp like the swordsman
giving up the fight,
would rise as the dented sword
with one last might

until my heart

stops racing,
and my mind is not so loud,
and I'd redo my stitches,

all but one.

Skin Deep

I was five years old, sitting in a field
knees folded among the dandelions,
wishes of whimsy floating by me

I didn't realize there were blades made of more
than grass there
I didn't realize the sharpest of stings could exist
in the soft earth

And the red trickled down my knee
before I realized I'd been stung
by a stray glass shard, glinting against the sun

I cried all the way home

I still don't know if it was from pain or from
fear,
but my mother was wise and knew the cure
and bandaged it right up

It was enough to stop my weeping

And yet, years later
I still roll up my pant leg
to see the raised scar just below my left knee,

a silent scream hidden within the skin

It asks me,
what makes pain more than skin deep?

Beauty Marks

Beauty marks my body
like a starlit city night
Not enough to trace any constellations,
but enough to know they're there

Below my right eyelashes
At the lower corner of my nose,
my mouth
Two dot my left hand
One at the base of my thumb
Above my knee, and at the center of my ankle,
amongst others sprinkled on my skin

They come with moles and skin tags and hair
and stretch marks
And together, they pave a path for me,
hidden treasures waiting to be revealed
at the times they're needed most

"Look here, what a lovely place to be
Let's make a home there
What mark shall we leave?"

I let the sun embrace my body
and shape me in their vision

I will not hide what the world makes of my
blank slate
I will revel in it
Cherish it
and let the metamorphosis of my body
be one
with that of my mind.

Glassy Eyes

I see your lies,
your glassy eyes
are telling me something different

You say you don't feel,
I know that's not real
The pain's something else,
                    now isn't it?

You say your heart's made of coal
Your mind's a black hole
Your soul's a sliver of its own self

I say, set fire to that coal
jump in that black hole
and I say
        -do it for your own self

I say...
(please look at me)

You're turning your head
your tongue's made of lead
you say your fucks are too few

I know that's not true
There's so much you rue
Now answer me dammit, why won't you?

You don't see this as healing
yet you're drunk with your feelings
and you'll close up once more when you're
sober

For your burdens, your lies
are in your glassy eyes
and they're starting to pour

right over.

At first sight

When my eyes first met yours
 there were no frozen frames,
fireworks,
frantic beats of the heart.
The world did not stop moving in the
magnificence
of two souls seeing one another for the first
time,

No.

When our eyes first met,
 it was quiet
Gentle as a wish nestled in a dandelion bud

It was the potential,
before the energy had a chance to form,
become kinetic

The pieces,
before they had a chance to be
connected

It was a moment,

a memory

It was you, meeting me
and-
me, meeting you
 and-
two people realizing another existed right at the
edge of their respective universes

For, love at first sight is simply
falling
          in
               love
with a story still to be written

The first kiss of ink to a page.

What we search for

Paint me an ocean
and let me wade in the pigment,
perhaps I'll drift to the island of you

I'll sing you a lullaby
neither soothing nor pleasant,
yet of my restless nights it will ring true

I don't know who you are,
perhaps I will or once did,
but can I trust you with words I've shared with
so few?

You don't know me at all
or perhaps all too well,
but are you lonely?

Are you looking?

Are you longing too?

Love and Found

If fear comes from the unknown,
can you call my name
when I forget myself?

If love comes from attention,
your voice will always carry
and I'll find you every time

You are the echo
of a dream long forgotten
You're the resonance of all that is good

I'll be your mirror
until you find it within
My gaze will reflect your divine.

The extent of our hearts

Your hands are rough
but your touch is kind,
and I wish I didn't hold on
long enough to learn

Your words are awkward
your thoughts are divine
For that incredible mind
I can't help but yearn

And your softest gaze
when your eyes meet mine
is a look that makes
my stomach churn

Because darling,
You say I'm the moon that is guiding your tides,
but you are the sun and I'm stealing your light
Don't act like you're nothing when you're
everything and more
don't see me as someone you can adore

For my hands are soft
but my grip is unsteady
I can't hold my own weight,
let alone carry yours

And my words are elegant
and vague and empty
My thoughts guarded
and made obscure

And my eyes look away
unsure, unready
The extent of your love
they cannot endure

Because darling,
My heart is full, but my mind is scared
for falling this hard, I was unprepared
I ache at the thought of letting you go
and I love you too much to let you know.

A Novel Experience

If you were a book then I'd be that passerby
who couldn't help but take a look,
and even though I would be rushing for some
errand or another,
I'd still reach out
and grab you by the collar and tug.

Entranced by that unique curve of your spine,
or was it that shade of your jacket?
or maybe something I couldn't see,
but like the invisible strings that pull our fate,
I would have been drawn to you.
And lifting you in my hands, I would have tried
to open you up,
wanting to be pulled into your world.

If you were a book, I'd be impulsive
and want to whisk you away.
Rather than carry you in my backpack of
knick-knacks,
I'd hold you by the hand,
feeling the company of our conversations
both told and still to be.

Something about that binding of yours

that makes you seem so composed.
Or maybe it is that the binding holds together
an unfathomable amount of wonder
that makes me want to know more.
And tell you tales of my own.

If you were a book then I'd be gentle
and treasure every word that comes out,
like the delicate dewdrop from a flower's petal
after a summer evening's rain.
I would cherish the way you whisper your
worries and joys,
your woven tales that make you.

Something about those lines of yours
that cannot be expressed in a better way,
or maybe it is those spaces of yours
between each phrase,
that hold their own little world to explore,
for another day.

If you were a book then I'd be sorry
about the times I'd have to leave.
For obligations write our tales,
as much as desire.
Yet I could never find a place in my bookshelf
for you,
a genre, sometimes thriller, or fantasy or humor
or mystery.

It's because of the changing tones that tie you
together,
like a bow of precipitation past.
Or maybe it's the fact that it's all you, all the
time.
and so I would place you by my bedside and
heart side
as my very own classic.

If you were a book then I'd be fearless
because of the faith I'd have
by having you by my side.
For no matter how many times my glance meets
yours,
and the times it doesn't, I'd know
that your stories go beyond that last page.

It's something about the way you stand
as your own genre, your story, your voice.
And maybe it's also the way you read me
like the first classic you've ever heard.

And it'd be a novel experience indeed.

Cosmic Evanescence

I heard you come before in a dream,
the tug of a memory
twice felt and once known

Your melody haunts me
in the sweetest of nightmares,
I can't tell if the tears
are from pain or from yearning

I saw you saunter in as if I was already yours,
as if I laid claim to your song before it was sung
As if for me it was sung

You were the breath falling from my lips
and you were the air seeping in my lungs
and the fact that you were is the greatest tragedy
because you were

and I still am

I felt you near and then I felt air
and I choked on my breath

because I couldn't bear it all

I couldn't bear it at all

Because you were the universe and I am a soul,
wandering
I belong to myself but I'm a part of you
and the world was more beautiful when I knew
you
so I open my eyes
and dream.

It was all for this

This ache from since I was aware of myself
and a thousand years before then
The yearning I feel in every pull of the wind
and in every fluttering leaf

The draw from tides of moonlight and salt tears
and from the horizon, tranquil and even
From the sinking sands embracing my presence
and the calling that dares not cease

And from loved ones and strangers and everyone
else
whenever I'm honest and raw,
I know not the language but feel the sentiment
whenever it finally rings true

I've hidden from myself for years and years
calling it my fatal flaw
But now I see, it's a welcome home
It was all for this
It was all for me

It was all to get to know you.

In You, I Believe

I believe in a kind God
who loved us into being
and as I rest my hands upon my chest
life pulsing with my breathing
I'm comforted in Your presence, All Knowing
and All Seeing

I believe in a fair God
who loves us as we are
and as I lay my forehead to the earth
my worries scatter far
for You who made every rock and star,
every being is on par

And I believe in a caring God
who loves us till the end
as I unfold my hands to speak with You
on Your grace I can depend

And, with love, all my fears I can transcend.